This journal belongs to

....

Contact Information

....

....

....

Date

....

Each day, *write something*
for which you are *thankful.*
When *God blesses you* in
special ways, write them down
so you *don't forget* them.

Introduction

One of the best ways to stay happy and positive is to keep a thankful heart and to say "Thank you" often. Negative feelings typically come from focusing on negative situations or thoughts. But when you remember how much you have to be grateful for, negativity will give way to optimism and hope.

I'm sure you can think of many creative ways to use this journal, but I'll make a few suggestions in case you're wondering how to get started. You may want to take time each day to jot down one thing—or anything you can think of—for which you are thankful. After a month, you will have at least thirty things you are thankful for, and if you have a disappointing or stressful day, you can reread your journal and feel encouraged.

You might also consider writing down your prayer requests. Then, when God answers them, record how He answered you, and simply write, "Thank You, Lord!" As you build a list of answered prayers, your faith and trust in God will grow stronger and stronger.

In addition, you may want to make note of any special or unexpected blessings God brings into your life. This way, you will remember that God knows what is meaningful to you and that sometimes He blesses you just because He wants to show you that He loves you.

I pray that this journal will become a treasure to you as it becomes a record of God's faithfulness in your life.

We are not born as thankful people, but we can cultivate
a culture of gratitude in our lives.

No matter what kind of difficulty we may face,
our blessings always outweigh our troubles.

Devote yourselves to prayer, being watchful and thankful.
Colossians 4:2

How many truly wonderful things would we recognize
in our lives if we would only take the time to look for them?

Because God does so much for us, we should be thankful in every circumstance, even if everything is not pleasant for us at the moment.

Gratitude and contentment go hand in hand; therefore, grumbling and discontentment must also go hand in hand.

When we pray, we don't have to try to sound spiritual or be in a certain posture; we simply need to be sincere.

Remaining thankful during difficulty is one way of waging effective spiritual warfare. When our enemy, Satan, attacks, he expects us to complain and focus on our problems instead of focusing on God and giving thanks to Him.

Give thanks to the LORD, for he is good; his love endures forever.
1 Chronicles 16:34

In the early stages of our relationship with God through Christ, we may not be aware of all the amazing ways He helps and blesses us on a regular basis; we may be more inclined to notice what we don't like about our lives and want God to fix.

Just think for a few minutes about the amazing privilege of being able
to go to the God who creates and maintains all things—
the God who loves you—and simply ask for His help.
Tell Him what you want or need.

Praying with thanksgiving doesn't simply mean thanking God during the prayer, but praying from the platform of a thankful life.

No matter how many annoying problems we have, God is still good and we are still blessed beyond understanding.

The giving of thanks is powerful beyond what we may realize.
It brings many benefits to our life and to the lives of other people.

We are not to be people-pleasers, but we are to be God-pleasers.

Let the peace of Christ rule in your hearts, since as members
of one body you were called to peace. And be thankful.
Colossians 3:15

Do you want to enjoy your life? If so, then it's necessary to keep your tongue free from evil, negative, and deceitful speech.

Complaints are nothing new. People throughout history have complained, but many of them turned their complaints into positive action.

We cannot complain our way into a better position in life.
If we are going to complain about something,
then we shouldn't bother praying about it.

Do not be anxious about anything, but in every situation,
by prayer and petition, with thanksgiving,
present your requests to God.

Philippians 4:6

In Ephesians 5:20, Paul pens these simple, yet powerful words:
"Always giving thanks to God the Father for everything,
in the name of our Lord Jesus Christ."

Thank you has power in it. It contains the power to encourage and to motivate a person to keep going, the power to lift them up and change what might have been a bad day into a good one.

If you don't like something, do something about it.

Are you letting opportunities to encourage others pass you by?

The Holy Spirit will inspire us with creative ways to bless people
if we will be sensitive and listen for His guidance.

Pride looks down on an individual it perceives as unimportant,
but humility lowers itself in order to lift others up.

And whatever you do, whether in word or deed,
do it all in the name of the Lord Jesus, giving thanks
to God the Father through him.

Colossians 3:17

We live in a world that seems to enjoy tearing people down.
We should be building people up, not putting them down.
Speaking words filled with death should not be
a habit among God's people.

Romans 14:19 teaches us that we must make an effort to edify
and encourage. This may not always come naturally,
but we can and should choose to do it regularly.

Complaining is a total waste of time, and it does no good at all.

I appreciate you," or "I'm glad you are in my life,"
are simple phrases that make a big impact.

One way to encourage people when they are hurting is to simply call or text to check on them. Just tell them you are thinking of them and wanted to check and see how they are doing.

Complaints open a door for the devil to work in our lives, but prayer with thanksgiving opens a door for God to work in our lives.

Devote yourselves to prayer, being watchful and thankful.
Colossians 4:2

Filling your day with the power of *thank you* improves your life immeasurably. It keeps you focused on the positive aspects of your life instead of the negative ones.

When we encourage someone, they often feel appreciated, and when we thank them for something, they feel encouraged.

Set a guard over my mouth, LORD; keep watch over the door of my lips.

Psalm 141:3

I challenge you to use your creativity to find ways to bless
the people around you.

Remember to thank God often for His love because
it is the greatest gift we have.

We should always seek God because He is wonderful,
good, kind, loving, merciful, and just plain awesome.

Our thoughts become our words, so if we are truly thankful,
I don't see how we can keep quiet about it.

Let us thank God daily for who He is and that He is in our lives,
inviting us into close, intimate relationship with Him through
our faith in Jesus Christ.

We have been set free from the tyranny of sin and guilt and from
the fear of being rejected by God. Even though He does not
approve of everything we do, He never stops loving us
and working with us to help us change and grow.

God's goodness provides our blessings, and being thankful
for those blessings allows us to keep them.

It is the Holy Spirit who changes us by the grace of God
as we submit our lives to Him to work in us.

Don't ever think that in God's eyes you are excused from helping people just because they don't deserve it.

When we seek first God's kingdom and His way of being and doing, He promises to add everything else to us that we need (Matthew 6:33).

Complaining is the fruit of a proud heart. When we complain, it means that we think we deserve better than what our circumstances have given us.

I will give thanks to the L<small>ORD</small> because of his righteousness;
I will sing the praises of the name of the L<small>ORD</small> Most High.

Psalm 7:17

The humble get the help, not the proud.

I believe that, as you experience the power of *thank you*, you will be amazed at the difference it makes in your life.

We don't want to let what was once a blessing to us become an expectation and a right.

Sometimes we are thankful out of the overflow of our hearts, and sometimes we have to remind ourselves to be thankful by looking back at how life used to be, compared to how it is now.

Let's always thank God for His goodness and remember
with grateful hearts all He has done for us.

An attitude of discontentment is part of our old nature, rather than part of the new nature God gives us when we are born again.

I will give thanks to you, Lord, with all my heart; I will tell of all your wonderful deeds. I will be glad and rejoice in you; I will sing the praises of your name, O Most High.

Psalm 9:1–2

When I stopped trying to collect from the people who could never repay me for the pain others had caused in my life, it allowed God to take over; He began healing me and blessing my life in ways that no one else could.

Our misery is the devil's greatest joy.

Let me encourage you to begin to cultivate a culture of thanksgiving in your life by going through your day being thankful for every blessing you have, especially the tiny ones that are easy to take for granted.

Our worth and value are found in Christ, not in our own abilities,
and we should always remember this.

If we truly believe we deserve nothing and are entitled to nothing,
I wonder how many things we previously felt we had a right
to would become things we are now thankful for.

We cannot be thankful without humility, and only through humility and gratitude will we find the desire to give generously to help those less fortunate than we are.

Βut thanks be to God! He gives us the victory through
our Lord Jesus Christ.

1 Corinthians 15:57

You only have one life to live, and God wants you to live wisely, be happy, and enjoy each day.

We should remember that Satan always opposes anything good and anything that brings progress.

Being thankful at all times in all situations is the right thing to do and will help us win our battles.

We can want change in the future while also being content with the present if we believe God's timing in our lives is perfect.

Greed steals our life; it prevents us from seeing our current blessings and has us focus only on what we want but do not have.

I wonder how often we lose our battles because we try to make things happen in our own strength when more gratitude and worship of God is what we really need.

....

....

....

....

....

....

....

....

....

....

....

....

....

....

....

....

....

....

....

....

....

A humble person will always be a thankful person.

Thanksgiving ushers in the presence of God,
and when God is present, we always have victory.

We often forget to be thankful for things that we have
all the time, and we tend to take them for granted.

Don't be jealous of what someone else has if you don't want
to do what they did to get it.

Being self-centered and happy at the same time is impossible.

I would like to be one of those amazing people who finds something to be thankful for, no matter how many difficulties I face, wouldn't you?

For I know the plans I have for you," declares the LORD,
"plans to prosper you and not to harm you,
plans to give you hope and a future."
Jeremiah 29:11

When we have God's presence, we have the answers to our problems and all the power we need to defeat our enemies.

When we are filled with thanksgiving, we guard our hearts against doubt and give God room to work in our lives:

Progress is amazing as long as we stay thankful for it.

Thanksgiving releases faith, hope, and joy, and it creates
an atmosphere for victory.

If we want to enjoy God's presence, we need to create an atmosphere in which He will be comfortable—one of peace, gratitude, and faith.

Praise be to the LORD, for he has heard my cry for mercy.

Psalm 28:6

As we continue seeking God, we grow spiritually
and learn what is truly important.

We are to give thanks at all times and in all situations.

God promises to heal our wounded souls, but this often requires our taking some God-inspired action—like giving thanks.

Let them give thanks to the LORD for his unfailing love
and his wonderful deeds for mankind.
Psalm 107:8

Silent gratitude doesn't do much for anyone.

We open a door to our enemy, the devil, through complaining.

When Paul wrote the letter to the Philippians, he was imprisoned and held in chains, yet he kept a good attitude.

Giving to others was one way the Israelites celebrated
and gave thanks for what God had done for them.

I urge you to fill your days with the power of *thank you* when it is easy and when it is hard and to be thankful for little things as well as big things.

But thanks be to God, who always leads us as captives in
Christ's triumphal procession and uses us to spread the aroma
of the knowledge of him everywhere.

2 Corinthians 2:14

We can easily see that gratitude is a weapon, but weapons
do us no good if we don't use them.

Focusing on what we have to be thankful for will prevent us from being faultfinders.

Part of what is wrong in the world is that most people
only see what is wrong.

When life is good and things are going our way, we find being thankful easy. But what about when life is hard?

Thankfulness is God's will.

Just imagine how situations could change if everyone was thankful in all circumstances and we heard praise and thanksgiving to God, instead of grumbling and complaining, on a regular basis.

One thing! Truly, there is only one thing that can keep us content. That is to keep God first in all we do, all the time.

Each of us must decide if we can be thankful for the rose
while dealing with the thorns.

We should always thank Jesus for His precious blood, with which we have been purchased and made God's own.

God wants us to trust Him, to know that anything we go through will work some good in our life, and to believe that when the trials are over, His goodness will prevent us from focusing on the thorns of life.

We cannot experience the power of *thank you*
unless we practice thinking and saying it.

I will praise you, Lord, among the nations; I will sing of you among the peoples. For great is your love, reaching to the heavens; your faithfulness reaches to the skies.

Psalm 57:9–10

It is easy to find fault with others, but in the process of doing so, we often forget about our own faults.

Words are containers for power, and we can choose the type of power we will put into them. This power can be positive in its ability to build up and encourage people or negative in its capacity to tear down and discourage them.

Focus on and highlight the good and positive things that God
does all the time to let us know that He is here,
that He loves us, and that He is still in control.

When what should be a blessing becomes a frustration,
I think we have a problem.

*S*o then, just as you received Christ Jesus as Lord, continue to live your lives in him, rooted and built up in him, strengthened in the faith as you were taught, and overflowing with thankfulness.

Colossians 2:6–7

Being thankful is so powerful that it will help
to heal your wounded soul.

The way we use our money says a lot about how thankful
we are for the life we have.

Always remember that we all have faults, but mercy is greater than judgment (James 2:13).

God's presence is everywhere because He is omnipresent;
He is never more than one thought away from us.

The devil wants to throw you in a pit and keep you there the rest of your life through resentment, hating the people who hurt you, but Jesus came to open prison doors and lift people out of hopelessness and despair.

God has delivered us, taking what Satan meant for harm
and working it out for our good.

I strongly encourage you to let today be a new beginning for you—
a place where you start fresh, letting go of what lies behind and
beginning anew with an attitude of gratitude and thanksgiving.

We can determine to derive some good out of everything
that comes our way.

An attitude of gratitude is beautiful.

It is important for us to talk about God's goodness as often as we can and to thank Him for all He has done, is doing, and will do in our lives.

Some of life's trials and tribulations are simply tests.
They test our faith and spiritual maturity.

*C*an you immediately think of a dozen blessings to be thankful
for without even making much of an effort?

....
....
....
....
....
....
....
....
....
....
....
....
....
....
....
....
....
....
....
....
....
....
....
....
....
....
....
....
....
....

God wants us to be abundantly blessed, but He won't give us material blessings that are beyond our spiritual maturity to manage well.

God is generous to us, and when we are generous to others,
we show that we are truly thankful for all He does for us.

I have developed the habit of always thanking God for Himself and for His presence in my life before I thank Him for all He does for me.

No one enjoys difficulty, but the less upset we become about it,
the easier it is to deal with.

We know we have victory over our difficulty before
the trial ever begins.

We have the ability to give people value with our words.

God is winking at you, but maybe you just need to open your
eyes and see your life from a little different perspective.

When we give thanks, we shift our focus away from our problems
and onto the answers.

Asking God for what we want without thanking Him for what
we have reveals a heart that is not right before Him,
perhaps a selfish or greedy heart.

God answers prayer, but He doesn't answer complaints.

Be content with what you have right now, knowing that God
has a perfect timing for the things you do not have yet.

The LORD is my strength and my defense; he has become my salvation.
He is my God, and I will praise him, my father's God, and I will exalt him.

Exodus 15:2

There is nothing bad that can happen to you that God
cannot turn into something good.

*T*hank you *has power in it.*

If you believe you may get what you ask, you will take time
to think before speaking.

What has God delivered you from? Take some time to think about what your life was like without Jesus in it.

Can you be satisfied with what God has given you at this time in your life?

_____

_____

_____

_____

_____

_____

_____

_____

_____

_____

_____

_____

_____

_____

_____

_____

_____

_____

_____

_____

_____

_____

_____

_____

_____

It is good to admire people, but we should never give them
the glory that belongs to God alone.

When we remain faithful and thankful during our trials, people notice and know that we belong to Jesus because we are displaying His character.

We should always be growing in godly character
and never be in decline.

Jesus died for us and took all the punishment we deserved as sinners, and He rose from the dead so that we might live a resurrection life and spend eternity with Him. This truth alone should be enough to keep us thankful all of our lives, even if we never have anything else.

....

....

....

....

....

....

....

....

....

....

....

....

....

....

....

....

....

....

....

....

....

....

....

In order to keep our blessings, we must keep
God first in our lives.

I always encourage myself and others to stand firm and pass the tests we face so we will not have to take them again.

Forming the habit of speaking words of gratitude
can greatly increase our happiness.

God's timing is always perfect.

Praise be to the God and Father of our Lord Jesus Christ,
the Father of compassion and the God of all comfort.

2 Corinthians 1:3

You don't have to wait for something good to happen to you before you start being generous.

God-winks are the little things that God does for us, which may
only be meaningful to us, but they let us know that
He is present and watching over us.

....
....
....
....
....
....
....
....
....
....
....
....
....
....
....
....
....
....
....
....
....
....
....
....
....
....
....
....
....

God takes the difficulties and mixes them with blessings,
and somehow it all works out well in the end.

Saying "thank you" doesn't cost anything.

Discontentment is an illness of the soul, but when we have
an attack of it, large doses of gratitude will heal it.

The greatest act of generosity the world has ever seen was when
God gave His only Son because of His love for us.
His actions teach us to give generously.

Develop and maintain a thankful heart, and you will be amazed
by the way God can use it for good.

Ask God for what you want and need, and then trust
His timing to be perfect in your life.

It is not happy people who are thankful,
it is thankful people who are happy.

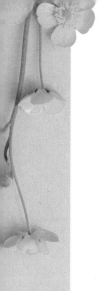

Ellie Claire
Hachette Book Group
1290 Avenue of the Americas, New York, NY 10104
ellieclaire.com

First Edition: January 2022

Ellie Claire is a division of Hachette Book Group, Inc. The Ellie Claire name and logo are trademarks of Hachette Book Group, Inc.

The publisher is not responsible for websites (or their content) that are not owned by the publisher.

Scriptures taken from the Holy Bible, New International Version®, NIV®. Copyright © 1973, 1978, 1984, 2011 by Biblica, Inc.™ Used by permission of Zondervan. All rights reserved worldwide. www.zondervan.com The "NIV" and "New International Version" are trademarks registered in the United States Patent and Trademark Office by Biblica, Inc.™

Print book interior design by Bart Dawson

ISBN: 9781546012474

Printed in Canada
MARQ-T
10 9 8 7 6 5 4 3 2 1